Selected Sermons

The Crossway Short Classics Series

The Emotional Life of Our Lord
B. B. WARFIELD

Encouragement for the Depressed
CHARLES SPURGEON

The Expulsive Power of a New Affection
THOMAS CHALMERS

Fighting for Holiness
J. C. RYLE

The Freedom of a Christian
MARTIN LUTHER

SELECTED
SERMONS

LEMUEL HAYNES

⠶ CROSSWAY®

WHEATON, ILLINOIS

Selected Sermons

Copyright © 2023 by Crossway

Published by Crossway
    1300 Crescent Street
    Wheaton, Illinois 60187

Cover design: Jordan Singer

Cover image: The Stapleton Collection / Bridgeman Images

First printing 2023

Printed in China

Unless otherwise indicated, Scripture quotations are from the *King James Version* of the Bible. Public domain.

Paperback ISBN: 978-1-4335-8196-0
ePub ISBN: 978-1-4335-8199-1
PDF ISBN: 978-1-4335-8197-7
Mobipocket ISBN: 978-1-4335-8198-4

Library of Congress Cataloging-in-Publication Data

Names: Haynes, Lemuel, 1753-1833, author.
Title: Selected sermons / Lemuel Haynes.
Description: Wheaton, Illinois : Crossway, 2023. | Series: The Crossway short classics series | Includes index.
Identifiers: LCCN 2022006187 (print) | LCCN 2022006188 (ebook) | ISBN 9781433581960 (trade paperback) | ISBN 9781433581977 (pdf) | ISBN 9781433581984 (mobi) | ISBN 9781433581991 (epub)
Subjects: LCSH: Haynes, Lemuel, 1753-1833—Sermons.
Classification: LCC BX7260.H315 A5 2023 (print) | LCC BX7260. H315 (ebook) | DDC 230.58092 [B]—dc23/eng/20220718
LC record available at https://lccn.loc.gov/2022006187
LC ebook record available at https://lccn.loc.gov/2022006188

Crossway is a publishing ministry of Good News Publishers.

RRDS   31 30 29 28 27 26 25 24 23
14 13 12 11 10 9 8 7 6 5 4 3 2 1

Contents

Foreword

YOU HOLD IN YOUR HANDS a rare gem recovered from one of the darker mines of church history, as Lemuel Haynes is perhaps the single most important American figure most Christians have never heard of. Born July 18th in 1753 to a Black man and a White woman, Haynes was abandoned by his parents in the home of a family friend who sold the infant Haynes into indentured servitude. By the providential hand of God, however, young Lemuel was placed into a Christian home, where by all accounts, including his own, he was treated as a member of the family and raised to love the things of God.[1]

Growing up in colonial Vermont, Haynes worked hard and studied hard, proving himself quite adept at intellectual pursuits despite being largely self-taught. He has affectionately been called a "disciple of the chimney-corner" as that is where he would spend most evenings after work reading and memorizing while other children were out playing or engaging in other diversions.

Haynes's commitment to theology began in that chimney-corner, and eventually he was born again. Not long after his conversion, he turned his followership of Christ and his intellectual bent into a serious endeavor by writing and preaching. An oft-told anecdote about Haynes concerns a

---

1   This foreword is adapted from Jared C. Wilson, "Lemuel Haynes and the Right Preaching of Justice," *For the Church* (blog), March 15, 2021, https://ftc.co/. Used by permission.

scene of family devotions at the Rose household where he was indentured. Given his adeptness at reading and his deep concern for spiritual matters, the Rose family would often ask Haynes to read a portion of Scripture or a published sermon. One night, Haynes read a homily of his own without credit (apparently the sermon on John 3:3 included in this volume). At the end, members of the family remarked at its quality and wondered, "Was that a Whitefield?" "No," Haynes is said to have replied, "it was a Haynes."

The few sermons we have of Lemuel Haynes prove him to be an exceptional expositor in the Puritan tradition, similar to Edwards or Whitefield though simpler than the former and more substantive than the latter. And yet, what Haynes may have lacked in eloquence compared to his contemporaries, he more than made up for in biblicism and applicational insight.

Officially licensed to preach in 1780 by the Congregational Association, Haynes soon after preached his first public sermon (on Psalm 96). He was then ordained in 1785 and would go on to receive an honorary Master of Arts degree from Middlebury College.

Haynes was a New Light revivalist and New Divinity theologian. He was also a patriot—he enlisted in the Continental Army in 1776 and marched with colonial troops to Ticonderoga, among other assignments. His military service was no mere distraction or aimless diversion but was representative of his heartfelt affection for the American experiment. His first biographer Timothy Mather Cooley thus described him by saying, "In principle he was a disciple of [George] Washington."[2]

---

2   Timothy Mather Cooley, *Sketches of the Life and Character of Rev. Lemuel Haynes* (New York: Harper & Brothers, 1837), 169.

These two significant truths about Haynes's philosophical convictions—his Puritan theology and his American patriotism—would prove to be the two most powerful motives in his life and ministry. He did not see these viewpoints as contradictory but complementary. Haynes believed, for instance, that the abolition of slavery was not just a true move of human righteousness in reflection of the real belief in the providence of God but also the truest form of faith in the American experiment.

So what kind of preacher was Lemuel Haynes? Cooley remarks, "Never did he wait to inquire whether a particular doctrine was popular. His only inquiries were, 'Is it true? Is it profitable? Is it seasonable?'"[3]

As such, Haynes ought to stand as a superlative model for modern American

3   Cooley, *Sketches*, 79.

evangelicalism—politically minded but theo-
logically driven—as he is indeed an ideologi-
cal forerunner for so many of the controversies
still peppering the evangelical landscape today.
For example, in his abolitionist tract "Liberty
Further Extended" (published in 1776!), one can
see clearly the theological and religious roots of
the concern for racial justice that one finds, for
instance, in Martin Luther King's "Letter from
a Birmingham Jail." In Haynes's work we find
a model for speaking to our divisive politico-
cultural contexts today. While we no longer
struggle with legalized slavery in America, we
are nevertheless still torn over issues of justice,
human relations, and other related concerns.
At once a Christian may feel drawn toward a
subgospel approach to justice issues, in which
doctrine takes a back seat to human flourishing
and liberation, and toward a nonapplicational

theology that divorces the gospel from its social implications.

Right now in American evangelicalism we are experiencing a great balkanization, some of which involves fracture lines along issues of social justice or racial reconciliation. One would think we'd be beyond the concerns addressed in more rudimentary terms in colonial America. But here we are, perennially in the place where our ministries must take the timeless word fearlessly and pastorally into a troubled world. Haynes can be a trusted guide in this endeavor.

In many ways, Haynes could be considered a kind of American Spurgeon—a faithful preacher and pastor, beloved for decades by his church and his family, and concerned to see the implications of the gospel fleshed out in homes and in society. Like Spurgeon, Haynes had a sharp wit and an imagist approach to illustration. Like Spurgeon's

own engagement with the Downgrade Controversy, Haynes maintained a regular public debate
with rising challenges to orthodoxy, including,
most notoriously, the universalist Hosea Ballou.
(His famous response to Ballou, allegedly preached
as an impromptu counterpoint immediately after
Ballou had soiled Haynes's own pulpit with this
heterodoxy, is titled "Universal Salvation" and included in this volume.) And like Spurgeon—thus
unlike some of his own ministerial contemporaries—Haynes needs no modern apologies, no
asterisk next to his legacy. He was a great minister
of grace, worthy of great emulation.

This is why I'm so grateful for Crossway's re-
publishing of this criminally overlooked American prophet. For nearly two hundred years, we
have received only two substantive biographies of
Haynes—the first, from Timothy Mather Cooley,
was published just four years after Haynes's death,

and the second, from historian John Saillant, was published in 2003 and is somewhat hard to find. The only published collection of Haynes's works is long out of print and extremely difficult to find. And since Haynes preached from outlines, many of which were apparently lost to the times, what endures of his work is both rare and precious. So, as I said, you hold a gem in your hands.

I trust you will find in these pages a sterling intellect and a careful theology, but also a passionate preacher of the gospel utterly besotted with the glory of God. Read and give thanks to God for Lemuel Haynes, and pray with me that the Lord will continue to raise up many more men of his kind.

Jared C. Wilson
Midwestern Baptist Theological Seminary

Series Preface

JOHN PIPER ONCE WROTE that books do not change people, but paragraphs do. This pithy statement gets close to the idea at the heart of the Crossway Short Classics series: some of the greatest and most powerful Christian messages are also some of the shortest and most accessible. The broad stream of confessional Christianity contains an astonishing wealth of timeless sermons, essays, lectures, and other short pieces of writing. These pieces have challenged, inspired, and borne fruit in the lives of millions of believers across church history and around the globe.

The Crossway Short Classics series seeks to serve two purposes. First, it aims to beautifully preserve these short historic pieces of writing through new high-quality physical editions. Second, it aims to transmit them to a new generation of readers, especially readers who may not be inclined or able to access a larger volume. Short-form content is especially valuable today, as the challenge of focusing in a distracting, constantly moving world becomes more intense. The volumes in the Short Classics series present incisive, gospel-centered grace and truth through a concise, memorable medium. By connecting readers with these accessible works, the Short Classics series hopes to introduce Christians to those great heroes of the faith who wrote them, providing readers with representative works that both nourish the soul and inspire further study.

Readers should note that the spelling and punctuation of these works have been lightly updated where applicable. Scripture references and other citations have also been added where appropriate. Language that reflects a work's origin as a sermon or public address has been retained. Our goal is to preserve as much as possible the authentic text of these classic works.

Our prayer is that the Holy Spirit will use these short works to arrest your attention, preach the gospel to your soul, and motivate you to continue exploring the treasure chest of church history, to the praise and glory of God in Christ.

Biography of
Lemuel Haynes

LEMUEL HAYNES (1753–1833) was one of the most extraordinary Christian preachers in American history. Born to an unknown White woman and African-American man, Haynes spent the first twenty-one years of life in indentured servitude. Immediately upon his release, Haynes joined the war effort against Great Britain, fighting at Lexington and Concord.

After the war, Haynes studied theology and became the first ordained Black preacher in the United States. He quickly became celebrated throughout New England for his scholarly yet passionate sermons, most of which he preached while pastoring a predominantly White church in Vermont.

Haynes's theological skill, rhetorical ability, and evangelical manner earned him the nickname "The Black Puritan." Convinced of Reformed theology and the sovereignty of God over all of life and history, Haynes wrote and preached to guide the hearts of his audience toward holiness, orthodoxy (especially against the heresy of universalism), and social reform.

Today, Haynes is celebrated both as a model of Reformed evangelical preaching and as an essential figure in the history of African-American Christianity.

UNIVERSAL

SALVATION

There is no greater folly than for men to express anger and resentment because their religious sentiments are attacked. If their characters are impeached by their own creed, they only are to blame.

All that the antagonists can say cannot make falsehood truth, nor truth, falsehood. The following discourse was delivered at Rutland, Vermont in June of 1805, immediately after hearing Mr. Ballou, a universal preacher, zealously exhibit his sentiments. The author had been repeatedly solicited to hear and dispute with the above preacher and had been charged with dishonesty and cowardice for refusing. He felt that some kind of testimony, in opposition to what he calls error, ought to be made, and has been urged to let the same appear in print. But whether, on the whole, it is for the interest of truth, is left to the judgment of the candid.

A SERMON

"And the serpent said unto the woman, Ye shall not surely die" (Gen. 3:4)

The holy Scriptures are a peculiar fund of instruction. They inform us of the origin of creation, of the primitive state of man, and of his fall, or apostasy, from God. It appears that he was placed in the garden of Eden with full liberty to regale himself with all the delicious fruits that were to be found, except what grew on one tree—

if he eat of that, that he should surely die, was the declaration of the Most High.

Happy were the human pair amidst this delightful paradise until a certain preacher, in his journey, came that way and disturbed their peace and tranquility by endeavoring to reverse the prohibition of the Almighty—as in our text, "Ye shall not surely die."

> She pluck'd, she ate.
> Earth felt the wound; nature from her seat.
> Sighing through all her works, gave signs
> of woe.
> That all was lost.

Milton[1]

We may attend to the character of the preacher, the doctrines inculcated, the hearer

---

1 Haynes is quoting John Milton's *Paradise Lost* (London: 1667).

addressed, and the medium or instrument of the preaching.

I. As to the preacher, I shall observe, he has many names given him in the sacred writings; the most common is the devil. That it was he who disturbed the felicity of our first parents is evident from 2 Corinthians 11:3 and many other passages of Scripture. He was once an angel of light and knew better than to preach such doctrine; he did violence to his own reason. But to be a little more particular, let it be observed:

1. He is an old preacher. He lived above 1,700 years before Abraham, 2,430 years before Moses, and 4,004 years before Christ. It is now 5,809 years since he commenced preaching. By this time he must have acquired great skill in the art.

2. He is a very cunning, artful preacher. When Elymas the sorcerer came to turn away people

from the faith, he was said to be full of all subtlety and a child of the devil, not only because he was an enemy to all righteousness, but on account of his carnal cunning and craftiness.

3. He is a very laborious, unwearied preacher. He has been in the ministry almost six thousand years and yet his zeal has not in the least abated. The apostle Peter compares him to "a roaring lion, walk[ing] about, seeking whom he may devour" (1 Pet. 5:8). When God inquired of this persevering preacher, "From whence comest thou?" he "answered the LORD, and said, From going to and fro in the earth, and from walking up and down in it" (Job 2:2). He is far from being circumscribed within the narrow limits of parish, state, or continental lines; his haunt and travel are very large and extensive.

4. He is a heterogeneous preacher, if I may so express myself. He makes use of a Bible when

he holds forth, as in his sermon to our Savior in Matthew 4:6. He mixes truth with error in order to make it go well or to carry his point.

5. He is a very presumptuous preacher. Notwithstanding God had declared, in the most plain and positive terms, "Thou shalt surely die" (Gen. 2:17), or "In dying, thou shalt die," yet this audacious wretch had the impudence to confront omnipotence and says "ye shall not surely die"!

6. He is a very successful preacher. He draws a great number after him. No preacher can command hearers like him. He was successful with our first parents, with the old world. Noah once preached to those spirits who are now in the prison of hell and told them from God that they should surely die, but this preacher came along and declared the contrary, "ye shall not surely die." The greater part, it seems, believed him and went to destruction. So it was with Sodom and

Gomorrah. Lot preached to them, the substance of which was, "Up, get you out of this place; for the LORD will destroy this city" (Gen. 19:14). But this old declaimer told them, "No danger, no danger, ye shall not surely die," to which they generally gave heed, and Lot seemed to them as one who mocked. They believed the universal preacher and were consumed (agreeably to the declaration of the apostle Jude), Sodom and Gomorrah and the cities about them, suffering the vengeance of eternal fire.

II. Let us attend to the doctrine inculcated by this preacher, "Ye shall not surely die." Bold assertion, without a single argument to support it! The death contained in the threatening was doubtless eternal death, as nothing but this would express God's feelings toward sin or render an infinite atonement necessary. To suppose it to be spiritual death is to blend crime and punishment together;

to suppose temporal death to be the curse of the law, then believers are not delivered from it, according to Galatians 3:13. What Satan meant to preach was that there is no hell and that the wages of sin is not death but eternal life.

III. We shall now take notice of the hearer addressed by the preacher. This we have in the text, "And the serpent said unto the woman." That Eve had not so much experience as Adam is evident; and so she was not equally able to withstand temptation. This doubtless was the reason why the devil chose her, with whom he might hope to be successful. Doubtless he took a time when she was separated from her husband.

That this preacher has had the greatest success in the dark and ignorant parts of the earth is evident: his kingdom is a kingdom of darkness. He is a great enemy to light. Saint Paul gives us some account of him in his day in 2 Timothy 3:6: "For of this sort are they which creep into houses, and lead captive silly women laden with sins, led away with divers lusts." The same apostle observes in Romans 16:17–18, "Now I beseech you, brethren, mark them which cause divisions and offences contrary to the doctrine which ye have learned; and avoid them. For they that are such serve not the Lord Jesus Christ, but their own belly; and by good words and fair speeches deceive the hearts of the simple."

IV. The instrument or medium made use of by the preacher will now be considered. This we have in the text, "And the serpent said." But how came the devil to preach through the serpent?

1. To save his own character, and the better to carry his point. Had the devil come to our first parents personally and unmasked, they would have more easily seen the deception. The reality of a future punishment is at times so clearly

impressed on the human mind that even Satan is constrained to own that there is a hell, although at other times he denies it. He does not wish to have it known that he is a liar; therefore he conceals himself that he may the better accomplish his designs and save his own character.

2. The devil is an enemy to all good, to all happiness and excellence. He is opposed to the felicity of the brutes. He took delight in tormenting the swine. The serpent, before he set up preaching universal salvation, was a cunning, beautiful, and happy creature; but now his glory is departed, for the Lord said unto the serpent, "Because thou hast done this, thou art cursed above all cattle, and above every beast of the field; upon thy belly shalt thou go, and dust shalt thou eat all the days of thy life" (Gen. 3:14). There is therefore a kind of duplicate cunning in the matter—Satan gets the preacher and hearers also.

And is not this triumphant flattery.
And more than simple conquest in the foe?
Young[2]

3. Another reason why Satan employs instruments in his service is because his empire is large and he cannot be everywhere himself.

4. He has a large number at his command who love and approve of his work, delight in building up his kingdom, and stand ready to go at his call.

INFERENCES

1. The devil is not dead but still lives and is able to preach as well as ever, "Ye shall not surely die."

2. Universal salvation is no newfangled scheme but can boast of great antiquity.

---

2   Haynes may be referring to Edward Young's *Night Thoughts on Life, Death, and Immortality* (London: 1743).

3. See a reason why it ought to be rejected: because it is an ancient devilish doctrine.

4. See one reason why it is that Satan is such an enemy to the Bible and to all who preach the gospel because of that injunction, "And he said unto them, Go ye into all the world, and preach the gospel to every creature. He that believeth and is baptized shall be saved; but he that believeth not shall be damned" (Mark 16:15–16).

5. See whence it was that Satan exerted himself so much to convince our first parents that there was no hell: because the denunciation of the Almighty was true, and he was afraid they would continue in the belief of it. Was there no truth in future punishment or was it only a temporary evil, Satan would not be so busy in trying to convince men that there is none. It is his nature and his element to lie. "When he speaketh a lie,

he speaketh of his own: for he is a liar, and the father of it" (John 8:44).

6. We infer that ministers should not be proud of their preaching. If they preach the true gospel, they only, in substance, repeat Christ's sermons; if they preach "Ye shall not surely die," they only make use of the devil's old notes that he delivered almost six thousand years ago.

7. It is probable that the doctrine of universal salvation will still prevail since this preacher is yet alive and not in the least superannuated and every effort against him only enrages him more and more and excites him to new inventions and exertions to build up his cause.

To close the subject: As the author of the foregoing discourse has confined himself wholly to the character of Satan, he trusts no one will feel himself personally injured by this short sermon. But should any imbibe a degree of friendship for this aged divine and think that I have not treated this universal preacher with that respect and veneration that he justly deserves, let them be so kind as to point it out, and I will most cheerfully retract, for it has ever been a maxim with me, "render [unto] all their dues" (Rom. 13:7).

A SERMON ON

JOHN 3:3

"Jesus answered and said unto him, Verily,
verily, I say unto thee, Except a man be born
again, he cannot see the kingdom of God."

John 3:3

THIS CHAPTER CONTAINS a conference between our blessed Lord and Nicodemus, a ruler of the Jews. This great man came to our Savior by night and addressed him in this manner: "Rabbi," says he, "we know that thou art a teacher come from God: for no man can do these miracles that thou doest, except God be with him" (John 3:2). Doubtless he had a rational conviction, from the many miracles that Christ did, that he was come from God. Our blessed Lord did not stand to show who he was but, like a wise and kind teacher, takes occasion to inculcate the importance of the great doctrine of regeneration and tells him, with a double asseveration, that except a man be born again he cannot see the kingdom of God. But, as great as this man was, we find that he was ignorant in a fundamental point in religion. It appeared a paradox unto him for he, supposing our Lord must mean a natural birth, asks him in verse 4, "How can a man be born when he is old? can he enter the second time into his mother's womb, and be born?" Christ, in order further to explain his meaning and to show that it was not a natural birth that he had reference to, adds, "Verily, verily, I say unto thee, Except a man be born of water and of the Spirit, he cannot enter into the kingdom of God" (v. 5). By this, perhaps, we may understand that as water is often made use of in the Scriptures as a symbolical representation of the regenerating and sanctifying influences of the Holy Spirit on the hearts of the children of men, so, unless we are born of the water of the Spirit (as divines interpret it), we cannot see the kingdom of God.

Our Lord proceeds to tell him, "That which is born of the flesh is flesh; and that which is born of the Spirit is spirit" (v. 6) as if to say, it would be to no purpose if a man should have another natural birth, seeing it would not alter his nature, for that which is born of the flesh is flesh—let it be born ever so many times of the flesh, it would still remain fleshly—and that which is born of the Spirit is spirit. "Marvel not that I said unto thee, Ye must be born again" (v. 7). And now it seemed a greater mystery to Nicodemus than ever; therefore he cries out in verse 9, "How can these things be?"

Thus you see, as I observed before, that although Nicodemus was a great man, a ruler of the Jews, he was ignorant about the new birth. And doubtless it is so now. There are many of the great ones of the earth—tell them about experimental religion, tell them that they must feel the Holy Spirit working powerfully on their hearts, that they must be born again, and they are ready to cry out, with this master in Israel, "How can these things be?"

But, to return to the words first read—in speaking something from these words I shall pursue the following method:

I. Show the necessity of regeneration, or of our being born again.

II. Explain the nature of the new birth, or what it is to be born again.

III. Show what we are to understand by seeing the kingdom of God.

IV. Make some remarks.

1. This will appear if we consider that state that mankind is in antecedent to the new birth. And

if we view human beings as they come into the world, we shall then find them haters of God, enemies to God, estranged from God, nay, the very heart is enmity itself against all the divine perfections; and we shall find them acting most freely and most voluntarily in these exercises. There is no state or circumstance that they prefer to the present, unless it be one whereby they may dishonor God more or carry on their war with heaven with a higher hand. They have no relish for divine things but hate, and choose to remain enemies to, all that is morally good. Now, that this is actually the case with sinners is very evident from the Scriptures. We are told in the chapter of which the text is a part that "that which is born of the flesh is flesh; and that which is born of the Spirit is spirit," which teaches us that there is nothing truly spiritual or holy in the first birth but that this comes by the second, or by the renewings of the Holy Ghost. Christ tells the Jews that they hated him without a cause. And the inspired apostle says that "the carnal mind is enmity against God: for it is not subject to the law of God, neither indeed can be. So then they that are in the flesh cannot please God" (Rom. 8:7–8). Therefore,

2. Seeing this is the state that human beings are in antecedent to the new birth, it is neither fit nor reasonable that God should bring them into favor with himself, or be at peace with them, without regeneration. Nay, he cannot, consistent with his perfection, for this would be for him to connive at wickedness when he tells us that he can "by no means clear the guilty" (Ex. 34:7). And

3. To suppose that sinners can see the kingdom of God or be happy in the divine favor without regeneration or the new birth is a perfect incon-

sistency, or contrary to the nature of the thing. The very essence of religion consists in love to God, and a man is no further happy in the favor of God than he loves God. Therefore, to say we enjoy happiness in God and at the same time hate God is a plain contradiction.

4. It is evident from Scripture that those to whom God gives a title to his spiritual kingdom are regenerated or born again and those who are not, and remain so, shall be miserable. This is not only asserted in the text by the Son of God, who was coequal, coeternal, and coessential with the Father, whose words stand more permanent than the whole fabric of heaven and earth and who stands at the gate of the universe and will not alter the things that have gone out of his mouth—I say, it was not only spoken by this glorious being who cannot lie, by his own lips, with a repeated "verily," but has been confirmed

by those whom he inspired and who, we are assured, had the mind of Christ. Saint Paul gives us the character of a good man, or one entitled to the heavenly world, in 2 Corinthians 5:17: "If any man be in Christ, he is a new creature: old things are passed away; behold, all things are become new." And they are said to be renewed in the spirit of their mind (Eph. 4:23; cf. Rom. 12:2) and to be born of God (John 1:13). And they are spoken of as being lovers of God (Prov. 8:17). And respecting those who are not of this character, or remain enemies to God, he tells us that he will pour out his fury upon them. Hence we read that "the wicked shall be turned into hell, and all the nations that forget God" (Ps. 9:17) and that "without [holiness] no man shall see the Lord" (Heb. 12:14). And Saint John the divine, having a view of the glory of the heavenly world, says that "there shall in no wise enter into it any thing that defileth, neither whatsoever worketh abomination, or maketh a lie: but they which are written in the Lamb's book of life" (Rev. 21:27). Thus we see the propriety of our Lord's assertion that "except a man be born again, he cannot see the kingdom of God" (John 3:3).

But, as I mean to handle the subject with the utmost brevity, I pass on,

II. To show the nature of regeneration, or what it is to be born again. And here,

1. I would consider the agent, or who it is that effects this great work. And if we consider that state that mankind is in by nature, as has been described above, we need not stand long to know who to attribute this work to. It is a work too great to attribute to men or angels to accomplish. None but he who, by one word's speaking, spake all nature into existence, can triumph over the opposition of the heart. This is the work of

the Holy Spirit, who is represented in Scripture as emanating from the Father and the Son, yet coequal with them both. It is God alone who slays the native enmity of the heart—who takes away those evil dispositions that govern the man, takes away the heart of stone and gives a soft heart—and makes him that was a hater of God, an enemy to God, to become friendly to his divine character. This is not wrought by any efficiency of man or by any external motives or by any light let into the understanding, but of God. Hence we read that those who receive Christ are "born, not of blood, nor of the will of the flesh, nor of the will of man, but of God" (John 1:13) and that it is the gift of God (Eph. 2:8)—also that it is "God which worketh in [us]" (Phil. 2:13).

Thus, I say, the man is entirely passive in this work; it is all wrought immediately by a divine agency.

In regeneration man is wholly passive; in conversion he is active. Regeneration is the motion of God in the creature; conversion is the motion of the creature to God, by virtue of that first principle whence spring all the acts of believing, repenting, and quickening. In all these man is active; in the other he is merely passive.

Charnock[1]

The man now becomes a new creature. Although he cannot discern what is the way of the spirit (as the wise man observes) or how God thus changes the heart, yet he knows that he has different feelings from what he had before. Therefore,

2. It is necessary that we consider those things that are the attendants or consequences of

---

1   Haynes is quoting Stephen Charnock's *A Discourse of the Nature of Regeneration* (Edinburgh: 1683).

regeneration or the new birth for there are no gracious or holy exercises that are prior thereto, to be sure, in the order of nature. Some seem to suppose faith to be before regeneration, but a little reflection upon the matter will show this to be wrong. By faith we are to understand a believing of those truths that God has exhibited in his word with a friendly heart. Now, to suppose that a man believes with this friendly heart antecedent to regeneration is to suppose that a man is a friend to God while in a state of unregeneracy, which is contradictory to Scripture. Now, if to believe with a friendly and right-disposed heart is absolutely necessary in order to constitute a true faith and such a heart is peculiar to the regenerate only, then we must be possessed with this heart (which is given in regeneration) before there can flow from it any such exercises, so that the man must become a good man, or be regenerated, before he can exercise faith or love or any grace whatever. Hence we read of men's receiving Christ and then becoming the sons of God (John 1:12). Therefore, what lies before us is to show what those fruits and effects are and what are those inward feelings that come in consequence of the new birth.

1. He loves God supremely. He loves holiness for what it is in itself because it agrees with his new temper; he chooses and prefers that to anything else. He loves the law of God. He loves the gospel and everything that is godlike. He loves the holy angels and the spirits of just men made perfect. His affections are set on things that are above. His treasure is there, and his heart will be there also. He loves the people of God in this world; nay, wherever moral rectitude is to be seen, he falls in love with it. He loves all mankind with a holy and virtuous love. Although he cannot love those who are the enemies of God with a love of complacency,

yet he loves them with the love of benevolence. He is of a noble and generous spirit. He is a well-wisher to all mankind. And this supreme love to God and benevolence to man is spoken of in Scripture as the very essence of true religion.

2. He repents of all his sins. He feels guilty before God. He sees and owns that God is right and he is wrong. He sees and gives in that it would be just for God to consign him over to the regions of despair. Now the man who could take no delight in anything else but sin hates it beyond anything whatever. Now he can acknowledge his sin with holy David, "Against thee, thee only, have I sinned"; "hide thy face from my sins, and blot out all mine iniquities" (Ps. 51:4, 9). He sees that "the sacrifices of God are . . . a broken and a contrite [heart]" (Ps. 51:17). Like the publican, afraid to look up, he smites upon his breast, saying, "God be merciful to me a sinner" (Luke 18:13).

3. He believes on the Lord Jesus Christ. I just observed what it was to believe. It is believing the record that God has given of his Son with a friendly heart. He gives in to the truths of the gospel with his heart, and he knows the truth by his own happy experience.

4. He is disposed to walk blameless in all the ordinances of God. He evidences by his holy walk that he has a regard for the honor of God. He endeavors to imitate his divine master in all his imitable perfections, knowing that "he that saith he abideth in him ought himself also so to walk, even as he has walked" (1 John 2:6). Oh, happy change indeed! The man is made like God in some good measure. He has the same kind of affections and dispositions as there are in God. He has a living principle within him that is active and vigorous, springing up into everlasting life.

But we pass on to take notice of the third thing in the method, which was

III. To show what we are to understand by seeing the kingdom of God.

Now we are not to suppose that it is an intuitive view that we have of the kingdom of God, as we behold objects with our eyes, but we are to understand enjoying or being admitted to possession of the blessings and entertainments of the heavenly world, or being brought into the divine favor. He cannot be a partaker of that unspeakable happiness that is in God; he cannot enjoy that blessed intercourse and holy communion that comes to the believer in consequence of his being united to Christ in this world or be admitted to those more sublime entertainments that are above. Something like this we are to understand by seeing the kingdom of God. But it will not be amiss to inquire a little what is meant by the kingdom of God. And we may understand

1. The spiritual kingdom of Christ here in this world—I mean that gracious temper of mind, or those holy dispositions that are implanted in the heart by regeneration, and also when a number of such do unite together in an ecclesiastical body. This is called Christ's kingdom because they not only have Christ's kingdom in their hearts, but also, being visibly united together to promote the cause of Christ, they may, by way of eminence, be so styled. And

2. We may understand the kingdom of glory, or this principle of divine life consummated in the heavenly world, so that this kingdom that believers have set up in them in this world is the same in kind as it is in heaven. But when we shall come to put off this tabernacle and be embodied spirits in the upper world, our love will be increased, and we

shall drink full draughts out of that crystal stream that glides gently through the paradise of God.

Oh, did believers once know adequately what is prepared for them in the heavenly world, how would they despise all things here below and long to be on the wing for heaven! Well may it be called a kingdom, where are crowns not of gold, but of glory—where the King of kings sits amid the heavenly throng and feeds them with his celestial dainties. And when the body is reunited to the soul at the resurrection, there will no doubt be much higher degrees of glory. Oh, then, let us live as becometh those who are so highly favored of the Lord!

APPLICATION

1. Hence see the propriety of our blessed Lord's assertion in the text that "except a man be born

again, he cannot see the kingdom of God" or enjoy the favor and love of God, either in this world or that to come. If men are totally depraved, as has been considered, from thence arises the absolute necessity of the new birth, and it is no strange or unaccountable thing that men must be born again. There is no obtaining the blessings of heaven without it. Therefore, says our Lord, "Marvel not that I said unto thee, Ye must be born again" (John 3:7).

2. Hence learn the folly of all those who rest in anything short of regeneration or the new birth, for however far we may go in the things of religion, yet if we are destitute of this divine and holy principle we may be assured of it, from Scripture as well as from the nature of things, that we cannot see the kingdom of God.

3. Let us examine ourselves whether we are possessed of this holy temper of heart or not. Have

we new dispositions, new affections, and new desires? Are God and divine things the center and object of our supreme love? Have we repentance toward God and faith in the Lord Jesus Christ? Have we got that universal benevolence that is the peculiar characteristic of a good man? Do we love the law of God? Have we viewed it in its purity and spirituality? Are we heartily disposed to walk in the ways of holiness? Do we freely and voluntarily choose that way? Are we well pleased with the gospel way of salvation?

4. Let all those who are strangers to the new birth be exhorted no longer to live estranged from God but labor after this holy temper of mind. Flee to Christ before it is too late. Consider that there is an aggravated condemnation that awaits all impenitent sinners. There is a day of death coming. There is a day of judgment coming. A few turns more upon the stage and we are gone. Oh, how

will you answer it at the bar of God for your thus remaining enemies to him? It is sin that separates from God. But it is the *being* or *remaining* such that will eternally separate you from him. Never rest easy till you feel in you a change wrought by the Holy Spirit. And believe it—until then you are exposed to the wrath of God, and without repentance you will in a few days be lifting up your eyes in torment.

The Lord grant that we may lay these things suitably to heart—that we, having the kingdom of Christ set up in our hearts here, may grow up to the stature of perfect men in Christ Jesus. This will lay a foundation for union with all holy beings, and with this, everlasting happiness in the kingdom of glory is inseparably connected through Jesus Christ our Lord. Amen.

THE CHARACTER
AND WORK OF
A SPIRITUAL
WATCHMAN
DESCRIBED

"For they watch for your souls,
as they that must give account."

Hebrews 13:17

NOTHING IS MORE EVIDENT than that men are prejudiced against the gospel. It is from this source that those who are for the defense of it meet with so much contempt. It is true—they are frail, sinful dust and ashes, in common with other men. Yet on account of the important embassy with which they are entrusted, it is agreeable to the unerring dictates of inspiration to "esteem them very highly in love for their work's sake" (1 Thess. 5:13).

To illustrate this sentiment was the delight of the apostle in this verse: "Obey them that have the rule over you, and submit yourselves" (Heb. 13:17). He was far from inculcating anything that might seem to confront what the apostle Peter has enjoined in 1 Peter 5:3, "Neither as being lords over God's heritage." The word signifies to *lead, guide,* or *direct* (Guyse's paraphrase).[1]

Our text contains an important motive—to excite to attention and respect what is due to the ministers of Christ on account of their relation to him, and that is the aspect their work has to a judgment day, "for they watch for your souls, as they that must quickly give account." They are amenable to their great Lord and Master for every sermon they preach and must give an account of the reception they and their work meet with among their hearers. Under the influence of such a thought, let us take notice of a few things supposed by the work assigned to ministers in the text and say something with respect to their

---

1   Haynes is quoting John Guyse's *The Practical Expositor: Or, an Exposition of the New Testament in the Form of a Paraphrase* (London: 1760).

character, whence it appears that they must give account, and when they may be said to be properly influenced by such considerations.

I. There are several ideas suggested by the work assigned to gospel ministers in the text, which is to watch for souls. This supposes

1. That the soul is of vast importance—else why is so much attention paid to it as to have a guard to inspect it? All those injunctions we find interpreted through the sacred pages to watchmen to be faithful are so many evidences of the worth of men's souls. What renders them so valuable is the important relation they stand in to their Maker. The perfections of the Deity are more illustrated in the redemption of fallen men than they would have been in the salvation of apostate angels—else why were the latter passed by while God chose the former as the objects of his attention? God has from eternity appointed a proper number,

for the display of his mercy and justice; means are necessary to fit them for the Master's use. So the soul in this view is of infinite importance.

2. "Watchmen over the souls of men" implies that they are prone to neglect them or to be inattentive to their souls. When one is set to inspect or watch over another, it supposes some kind of incapacity that he is under to take care of himself. The Scripture represents mankind by nature as fools, madmen, and being in a state of darkness.

Men in general are very sagacious with respect to temporal affairs and display much natural wit and ingenuity in contriving and accomplishing evil designs, but "to do good they have no knowledge" (Jer. 4:22). This is an evidence that their inability to foresee danger, and provide against it, is of the moral kind. Was there a disposition in human beings, correspondent to their natural powers, to secure the eternal interest of their souls in the way God has prescribed, watchmen would in a great measure be useless.

3. The work and office of gospel ministers suggest the idea of enemies invading—that there is a controversy subsisting and danger approaching. When soldiers are called forth and sentinels stand upon the wall, it denotes war. The souls of men are environed with ten thousand enemies who are seeking their ruin. Earth and hell are combined together to destroy. How many already have fallen victims to their ferocity! The infernal powers are daily dragging their prey to the prison of hell. Men have rebelled against God and made him their enemy; yea, all creatures and all events are working the eternal misery of the finally impenitent sinner.

4. We are taught in the text and elsewhere that the work of a gospel minister is not with the temporal but with the spiritual concerns of men: they

watch for *souls*. Their conversation is not to be about worldly affairs but about things that relate to Christ's kingdom, which involves the everlasting concerns of men's souls. When a minister's affections are upon this world, his visits among his people will be barren; he will inquire about the outward circumstances of his flock and perhaps, from pecuniary motives, rejoice at such prosperity. But as though that was of greatest concern, he will have nothing to say with respect to the health and prosperity of their souls, have no joys or sorrows to express on account of the fruitful or more lifeless state of the inward man.

II. Let us say something with respect to the character of a spiritual watchman.

Natural endowments embellished with a good education are qualifications so obviously requisite in an evangelical minister that it is needless we insist upon them at this time; and that the interest of religion has, and still continues, greatly to suffer for the want of them is equally notorious.

In the early ages of Christianity, men were miraculously qualified and called into the work of the gospel ministry; but we are far from believing that this is the present mode by which ordinary ministers are introduced.

1. It is necessary that those who engage in this work love the cause on which they profess to be embarked, that the love of Christ be shed abroad in the heart. Hence our blessed Lord, by whose repeated interrogations to Simon whether he loved him, has set before us the importance of this qualification in a spiritual shepherd. The sad consequences of admitting those into the army who are in heart enemies to the commonwealth have often taught men to be careful in this particular. The trust reposed in a watchman is such as renders him capable of great detriment to the community.

He that undertakes in this work from secular motives will meet with disappointment. What a gross absurdity is this, for a man to commend religion to others while he is a stranger to it himself! "The pious preacher will commend the Savior from the personal fund of his own experience."[2] Being smitten with the love of Christ himself, with what zeal and fervor will he speak of the divine glory! Love to Christ will tend to make a minister faithful and successful. The importance of this point urges me to be copious on the subject, were it not too obvious to require a long discussion.

2. Wisdom and prudence are important qualifications in ministers—hence that injunction of the great preacher, "Be ye therefore wise as serpents, and harmless as doves" (Matt. 10:16). He is a man of spiritual understanding whose

---

2 Haynes has adapted a quotation from James Fordyce's "The Eloquence of the Pulpit, An Ordination Sermon" (Aberdeen: 1752).

soul is irradiated with the beams of the Son of Righteousness, who has received an unction from the Holy One, is taught by the word and Spirit, and walks in the light of God's countenance. He has seen the deceit of his own heart, knows the intrigues of the enemy, sees the many snares to which the souls of men are exposed, and, not being ignorant of the devices of Satan, he will endeavor to carry on the spiritual campaign with that care and prudence that Satan shall not get advantage. He knows that he has a subtle enemy to oppose and also human nature, replete with enmity against the gospel, and will endeavor, in every effort, to conduct with that wisdom and circumspection as shall appear most likely to prove successful.

3. Patience is another qualification very necessary in a spiritual watchman. His breast being inspired with love to the cause, he will stand the

storms of temptation and will not be disheartened by all the fatigues and sufferings to which his work exposes him but will endure hardness as a good soldier of Jesus Christ.

4. Courage and fortitude must constitute a part of the character of a gospel minister. A sentinel who is worthy of that station will not fear the formidable appearance of the enemy nor tremble at their menaces. None of these things will move him, neither will he count his life too dear unto him to defend a cause so very important. He has the spirit of the intrepid Nehemiah: "Should such a man as I flee?" (Neh. 6:11). He stands fast in the faith, quits himself like a man, and is strong (1 Cor. 16:13).

5. Nor must we forget to mention vigilance, or close attention to the business assigned him, as an essential qualification in a minister of Christ. A man does not answer the idea of a watchman unless his mind is engaged in the business. The

word that we have rendered *watch* in the text signifies, in the original, to awake and abstain from sleeping (Leigh's *Critica Sacra*).[3] Indeed, all the purposes of a watch set upon the wall are frustrated if he sleeps on guard; thereby himself and the whole army are liable to fall an easy prey to the cruel depredations of the enemy. The spiritual watchman is not to sleep but to watch for the first motion of the enemy and give the alarm, lest souls perish through his drowsiness and inattention.

Some further observations with respect to the work of a gospel minister will be made in their place. We pass

III. To show that ministers must give account to God of their conduct, especially as it respects the people of their charge.

---

3   Haynes is quoting Edward Leigh's *Critica Sacra: Or, Philological and Theological Observations, Upon All the Greek Words of the New Testament, in Order Alphabetical* (London: 1639).

This solemn consideration is suggested in the text below. It is the design of preaching to make things ready for the day of judgment. "To the one we are the savour of death unto death; and to the other the savour of life unto life" (2 Cor. 2:16). We are fitting men for the Master's use, preparing affairs for that decisive court. This supposes that things must be laid open before the great assembly at the day of judgment—or why is it that there are so many things that relate thereto and are preparatives therefore?

The work of a gospel minister has a peculiar relation to futurity: an approaching judgment is that to which every subject is pointing and which renders every sentiment to be inculcated vastly solemn and interesting. Ministers are accountable creatures in common with other men; and we have the unerring testimony of Scripture that "God shall bring every work into judgment, with every secret thing, whether it be good, or whether it be evil" (Eccl. 12:14). If there is none of our conduct too minute to be cognizable, we may well conclude that such important affairs that relate to the work and office of gospel ministers will not pass unnoticed.

Arguments may be taken from the names given to the ministers of Christ to show that they must give account. They are called soldiers, ambassadors, servants, stewards, and angels, which points out the relation they and their work stand in to God—that they are sent of God and are amenable to him who sent them, just as a servant or steward is to give account to his lord and master with respect to his faithfulness in the trust reposed in him. God tells Ezekiel that if watchmen are not faithful and souls perish through their neglect, he would require their blood at the hands of such careless watchmen. It is evident that primitive ministers were influenced to faithfulness from a view of the solemn account they expected to give at the day of judgment. This gave rise to those words, "But Peter and John answered and said unto them, Whether it be right in the sight of God to hearken unto you more than unto God, judge ye" (Acts 4:19). If God's omniscience is a motive to faithfulness, it must be in this view: that he will not let our conduct pass unnoticed but call us to an account.

It was approaching judgment that engrossed the attention of Saint Paul and made him exhort Timothy to study to approve himself unto God. This made the beloved disciple speak of having "boldness in the day of judgment" (1 John 4:17).

The divine glory is an object only worthy of attention, and to display his holy character was the design of God in creation, as there were no other beings existing antecedent thereto to attract the mind of Jehovah. And we are sure that God is pursuing the same thing still, and always will. "He is of one mind, and who can turn him?" (Job 23:13). There is no conceivable object that bears any proportion with the glory of God, and for him ever to aim at anything else would be incompatible with his perfections. The day of judgment is designed to be a comment on all other days, at which time God's government of the world and their conduct toward him will be publicly investigated, that the equity of divine administration may appear conspicuous before the assembled universe. It is called a day when the son of man is "revealed" (Luke 17:30). The honor of God requires that matters be publicly and particularly attended to, that evidences are summoned at this open court: hence the saints are to "judge the world" (1 Cor. 6:2).

It will conduce to the mutual happiness of faithful ministers and people to have matters laid open before the bar of God, as in the words following our text, that they may do it with "joy, and not with grief" (Heb. 13:17). The apostle speaks of some ministers and people who should have reciprocal joy in the day of the Lord Jesus, which supposes that ministers and the people of their charge are to meet another day as having something special with each other. The connection between ministers and people is such as renders them capable of saying much for or against the people of their charge and of hearers making the same observations with respect to their teachers; and in this way the mercy and justice of God will appear illustrious.

Since, therefore, the work of gospel ministers has such a near relation to a judgment day, since they are accountable creatures and their work so momentous, since it is a sentiment that has had so powerful influence on all true ministers in all ages of the world—also their connection is such as to render them capable of saying many things relating to the people of their charge—above all, since the displays of divine glory are so highly concerned in this matter, we may without hesitation adopt the idea in the text that ministers have a solemn account to give to their great Lord and Master how they discharge the trust reposed in them.

IV. We are to inquire what influence such considerations will have on the true ministers of Christ or when they may be said to preach and act as those who must give account.

1. Those who properly expect to give account will be very careful to examine themselves with respect to the motives by which they are influenced to undertake in this work. He will view himself acting in the presence of

a heart-searching God who requires truth in the inward part and will shortly call him to an account for all the exercises of his heart. He will search every corner of his soul as to whether the divine honor or something else is the object of his pursuit. He has been taught by the rectitude of the divine law that God will not pass by transgressors but will judge the secrets of men. The work will appear so great that nature will recoil at the thought like Jeremiah, "Ah, Lord GOD! behold, I cannot speak: for I am a child," or with the great apostle, "Who is sufficient for these things?" (Jer. 1:6; 2 Cor. 2:16). The true disciple of Jesus will not thrust himself forward into the ministry like a heedless usurper but with the greatest caution and self-diffidence.

2. A faithful watchman will manifest that he expects to give account by being very careful to know his duty and will take all proper ways that

are in his power to become acquainted with it. He will study, as the apostle directs Timothy, to show himself "approved unto God" (2 Tim. 2:15). He will give attendance to reading, meditation, and prayer and will often call in divine aid on account of his own insufficiency. As a faithful soldier will be careful to understand his duty, so the spiritual watchman will adhere closely to the word of God for his guide and directory.

3. A minister who watches for souls as one who expects to give account will have none to please but God. When he studies his sermons, this will not be the inquiry, "How shall I form my discourse so as to please and gratify the humors of men and get their applause?" but "How shall I preach so as to do honor to God and meet with the approbation of my Judge?" This will be his daily request at the throne of grace. This will be ten thousand times better to him than the vain

flattery of men. His discourses will not be calculated to gratify the carnal heart, and he will not shun to declare the whole counsel of God.

The solemn account that the faithful minister expects to give another day will direct him in the choice of his subjects. He will dwell upon those things that have a more direct relation to the eternal world. He will not entertain his audience with empty speculations or vain philosophy but with things that concern their everlasting welfare. Jesus Christ and him crucified will be the great topic and darling theme of his preaching. If he means to save souls, like a skillful physician he will endeavor to lead his patients into a view of their maladies and then point them to a bleeding Savior as the only way of recovery. The faithful watchman will give the alarm at the approach of the enemy, will blow the trumpet in the ears of the sleeping sinner and endeavor to awake him.

4. The pious preacher will endeavor to adapt his discourses to the understanding of his hearers. "He will not be ambitious of saying fine things to win applause, but of saying useful things, to win souls."[4] He will consider that he has the weak as well as strong, children as well as adults to speak to, and that he must be accountable for the blood of their souls if they perish through his neglect. This will influence him to study plainness more than politeness. Also, he will labor to accommodate his sermons to the different states or circumstances of his hearers; he will have comforting and encouraging lessons to set before the children of God, while the terrors of the law are to be proclaimed in the ears of the impenitent. He will strive to preach distinguishingly, that

4   Haynes is quoting James Fordyce's "The Eloquence of the Pulpit, An Ordination Sermon" (Aberdeen: 1752).

every hearer may have his portion. The awful scenes of approaching judgment will have an influence on the Christian preacher with respect to the manner in which he will deliver himself. He will guard against that low and vulgar style that tends to degrade religion; but his language will in some measure correspond with those very solemn and affecting things that do engage his heart and tongue. He will not substitute a whining tone in the room of a sermon, which, to speak no worse of it, is a sort of satire upon the gospel, tending greatly to depreciate its solemnity and importance and to bring it into contempt; but the judgment will appear so awful, and his attention so captivated with it, that his accents will be the result of a mind honestly and engagedly taken up with a subject vastly important. "Such a preacher will not come into the pulpit, as an actor comes upon the stage, to personate a feigned character, and forget his real one, to utter sentiments, or represent passions not his own" (Fordyce).[5] It is not to display his talents. Like one who feels the weight of eternal things, he will not address his hearers as though judgment was a mere empty sound, but viewing eternity just before him and a congregation on the frontiers of it, whose eternal state depends upon a few uncertain moments, oh, with what zeal and fervor will he speak! How will death, judgment, and eternity appear as it were in every feature and every word! Out of the abundance of his heart, his mouth will speak. His hearers will easily perceive that the preacher is one who expects to give account. He will study and preach with reference to a judgment to come and deliver

5 Haynes is quoting James Fordyce's "Eloquence of the Pulpit."

every sermon, in some respects, as if it were his last, not knowing when his Lord will call him or his hearers to account. We are not to suppose that his zeal will vent itself in the frightful bellowings of enthusiasm; but he will speak forth the words of truth in soberness, with modesty and Christian decency.

5. They who watch for souls as those who expect to give account will endeavor to know as much as may be the state of the souls committed to their charge that they may be in a better capacity to do them good. They will point out those errors and dangers they may see approaching; and when they see souls taken by the enemy, they will exert themselves to deliver them from the snare of the devil. The outward deportment of a faithful minister will correspond with his preaching: he will reprove and rebuke, warning his people from house to house. The weighty

affairs of another world will direct his daily walk and conversation in all places and on every occasion.

A FEW PARTICULAR ADDRESSES

First, to him who is about to be set apart to the work of the gospel ministry in this place:

Dear sir, from the preceding observations you will easily see that the work before you is great and solemn. And I hope this is a lesson you have been taught otherwise; the former acquaintance I have had with you gives me reason to hope that this is the case. You are about to have these souls committed to your care; you are to be placed as a watchman upon the walls of this part of Zion. I doubt not but that it is with trembling you enter upon this work. The relation that this day's business has with a judgment to come renders the scene affecting. Your mind, I trust, has already anticipated the important moment when you must meet this people before the bar of God. The good profession you are this day to make is before many witnesses. Saints and wicked men are beholding. The angels are looking down upon us. Above all, the great God, with complacency or disapprobation, beholds the transactions of this day; he sees what motives govern you and will proclaim it before the assembled universe. Oh, solemn and affecting thought! The work before you is great and requires great searching of heart, great self-diffidence and self-abasement. How necessary that you feel your dependance upon God; you cannot perform any part of your work without his help. Under a sense of your weakness, repair to him for help. Would you be a successful minister, you must be a praying, dependant one: do all in the name and strength of the Lord Jesus. Would you be faithful in watching for the souls of men, you must be much in watching your own heart. If you are careless with respect to your own soul, you will be also with respect to others. Although the work is too great for you, yet let such considerations as these revive your desponding heart: that the cause is good, better than life, so you may well give up all for it; it is the cause of God that will prove victorious in spite of all opposition from men or devils; God has promised to be with his ministers to the end of the world; the work is delightful (Paul somewhere blesses God for putting him into the work of the ministry); the campaign is short (your warfare will soon be accomplished); and the reward is great (being found faithful, you will receive a crown of glory that fadeth not away).

Secondly, we have a word to the church and congregation in this place.

My brethren and friends, the importance of the work of a gospel minister suggests the weighty concerns of your souls. As ministers must give account of how they preach and behave, so hearers also are to be examined how they hear and improve. You are to hear with a view to the day of judgment, always remembering that there is no sermon or opportunity that you have in this life to prepare for another world that shall go unnoticed at that decisive court. Your present exercises, with respect to the solemn affairs of this day, will then come up to public view.

God, we trust, is this day sending you one to watch for your souls; should not this excite sentiments of gratitude in your breasts? Shall God take so much care of your souls and you neglect them? How unreasonable will it be for you to despise the pious instruction of your watchmen! You will herein wrong your own souls, and it will be an evidence that you love death. You will bear with him in not accommodating his sermons to your vitiated tastes because he must give account. His work is great, and you must pray for him, as in the verse following the text, where the apostle says, "Brethren, pray for us" (Heb. 13:18). Since it is the business of your minister to watch for your souls with such indefatigable assiduity, you easily see how necessary it is that you do what you can to strengthen him in this work and that you administer to his temporal wants so that he may give himself wholly to these things. The great backwardness among people in general with respect to this matter at present has an unfavorable aspect: "Who goeth a warfare any time at his own charges? who planteth a vineyard, and eateth not of the fruit thereof? or who feedeth a flock, and eateth not of the milk of the flock" (1 Cor. 9:7).

Doubtless this man is sent here for the rise and fall of many in this place. We hope he will be used as a means of leading some to Christ, while on the other hand, we even tremble at the thought that he may fit others for a more aggravated condemnation. Take heed how you hear.

A FEW WORDS TO THE ASSEMBLY IN GENERAL WILL CLOSE THE SUBJECT

What has been said about the character and work of gospel ministers shows us at once that it is a matter in which we are all deeply interested. The greater part of the people present I expect to see no more until I meet them at that day that has been the main subject of the foregoing discourse. With respect to the characters of the people present, we can say but little about them; only this we may observe—they are all dying creatures, hastening to the grave and to judgment! There must we meet you; there an account of this day's work will come up to view; there each one must give account concerning the right discharge of the work assigned him! The preacher must give account, and you that hear also. Let me say to such as are yet in their sins and proclaim it from this part of the wall of Zion that the enemy of your souls is at hand, that destruction awaits you. Oh, flee, flee to Christ Jesus! Bow to his sovereignty. Know this, that except you are born again and become new creatures in the dispositions of your mind, you cannot be saved. Shall ministers watch and pray for your souls night and day and you pay no attention to them? Since they are so valuable, having such a relation to God, did men regard divine glory, they would regard their souls as being designed to exhibit it. Be instructed, then, to delay no longer, but by repentance toward God and faith in the Lord Jesus Christ, make peace with him before you are summoned before his awful bar. Let me bear testimony against a practice too common on such occasions as this: many people think it a time for carnal mirth and dissipation, than which nothing can be more provoking to God nor inconsistent with that day and the strict account that such an occasion tends to excite in the mind. May all, both ministers and people, be exhorted to diligence in their work, that finally we may adopt the language of the blessed apostle, "As also ye have acknowledged us in part, that we are your rejoicing, even as ye also are ours in the day of the Lord Jesus" (2 Cor. 1:14). Amen.

LIBERTY FURTHER

EXTENDED

Or Free Thoughts on the Illegality
of Slave Keeping, Wherein Those
Arguments that Are Used in its
Vindication Are Plainly Confuted,
Together with a Humble Address to
Such As Are Concerned in the Practice.

*"We hold these truths to be self-evident,
that all men are created equal, that they
are Endowed by their Creator with certain
unalienable rights, that among these are
Life, Liberty, and the pursuit of Happiness."*

Congress

AS TYRANNY HAD ITS ORIGIN from the infernal regions, so it is the duty and honor of every son of freedom to repel her first motions. But while we are engaged in the important struggle, it cannot be thought impertinent for us to turn one eye into our own breast for a little moment and see whether through some inadvertency or a self-contracted spirit we do not find the monster lurking in our own bosom, that now while we are inspired with so noble a spirit and becoming zeal, we may be disposed to tear her from us. If the following would produce such an effect, the author should rejoice.

It is evident, by ocular demonstration, that man by his depravity has procured many corrupt habits that are detrimental to society. And although there is a way prescribed whereby man may be reinstated into the favor of God, yet these corrupt habits are not extirpated, nor can the subject of renovation boast of perfection, till he leaps into a state of immortal existence. Yet it has pleased the majesty of heaven to exhibit his will to men and endow them with an intellect that is susceptible of speculation. Yet, as I observed before, man, in consequence of the fall, is liable to digressions. But to proceed.

Liberty and freedom are innate principles that are unmovebly placed in the human species, and to see a man aspire after them is not enigmatical, seeing he acts no ways incompatible with his own nature. Consequently, he who would infringe upon a man's liberty may reasonably expect to meet with opposition, seeing the defendant cannot comply to nonresistance unless he counteracts the very laws of nature.

Liberty is a jewel that was handed down to man from the cabinet of heaven and is coequal with his existence. And as it proceeds from the supreme legislature of the universe, so it is he who has a sole right to take it away. Therefore, he that would take away a man's liberty assumes a prerogative that belongs to another and acts out of his own domain.

One man may boast a superiority above another in point of natural privilege; yet if he can produce no convincing arguments in vindication of this preeminence, his hypothesis is to be suspected. To affirm that an Englishman has a right to his liberty is a truth that has been so clearly evinced, especially of late, that to spend time in illustrating this would be but superfluous tautology. But I query whether liberty is so contracted a principle as to be confined to any nation under heaven; nay, I think it not hyperbolical to affirm that even an African has equally as good a right to his liberty in common with Englishmen.

I know that those who are concerned in the slave trade do pretend to bring arguments in vindication of their practice; yet if we give them a candid examination, we shall find them (even those of the most cogent kind) to be essentially deficient. We live in a day wherein liberty and freedom are the subjects of many millions' concern, and the important struggle has already caused great effusion of blood. Men seem to manifest the most sanguine resolution not to let their natural rights go without their lives go with them—a resolution, one would think, everyone that has the least love for his country or future posterity would fully confide in. Yet while we are so zealous to maintain and foster our own invaded rights, it cannot be thought impertinent for us to candidly reflect on our own conduct, and I doubt not but that we shall find that subsisting in the midst of us that may with propriety be styled *oppression*, nay, much greater oppression than that which Englishmen seem so much to spurn at. I mean an oppression that they themselves impose upon others.

It is not my business to inquire into every particular practice that is practiced in this land that may come under this odious character. But what I have in view is humbly to offer some free thoughts on the practice of slave keeping. Oppression is neither spoken of nor ranked in the sacred oracles among the least of those sins that are the procuring cause of those signal judgments that God is pleased to bring upon the children of men. Therefore let us attend. I mean to write with freedom, yet with the greatest submission.

And the main proposition that I intend for some brief illustration is this, namely, that an African— or, in other terms, that a Negro—may justly challenge and has an undeniable right to his freedom and liberty. Consequently, the practice of slave keeping that so much abounds in this land is illicit.

Every privilege that mankind enjoys has its origin from God, and whatever acts are passed in any earthly court that are derogatory to those edicts that are passed in the court of heaven, the act is void. If I have a particular privilege granted to me by God and the act is not revoked nor the power that granted the benefit vacated (as it is impossible but that God should ever remain immutable), then he who would infringe upon my benefit assumes an unreasonable and tyrannic power.

It has pleased God to "ma[k]e of one blood all nations of men for to dwell on all the face of the earth" (Acts 17:26). And as all are of one species, so there are the same laws and aspiring principles placed in all nations; and the effects that these laws will produce are similar to each other. Consequently, we may suppose that what is precious to one man is precious to another, and what is irksome or intolerable to one man is so to another, considered in a law of nature. Therefore we may reasonably conclude that liberty is equally as precious to a Black man as it is to a White one, and bondage equally as intolerable to the one as it is to the other, seeing as it affects the laws of nature equally as much in the one as it does in the other. But, as I observed before, those privileges that are granted to us by the Divine Being, no one has the least right to take from us without our consent; and there is not the least precept or practice in the sacred Scriptures that constitutes a Black man a slave any more than a White one.

Shall a man's color be the decisive criterion whereby to judge of his natural right? Or, because a man is not of the same color with his neighbor, shall he be deprived of those things that distinguish him from the beasts of the field?

I would ask, whence is it that an Englishman is so far distinguished from an African in point of natural privilege? Did he receive it in his original constitution? Or by some subsequent grant? Or does he boast of some higher descent that gives him this preeminence? For my part I can find no such revelation. It is a lamentable consequence of the fall that mankind has an insatiable thirst after superiority one over another, so that however common or prevalent the practice may be, it does not amount, even to a circumstance, that the practice is warrantable.

God has been pleased to distinguish some men from others as to natural *abilities* but not as to natural *right* as they came out of his hands. But sometimes men by their flagitious practice forfeit their liberty into the hands of men by becoming unfit for society. But have the Africans ever as a nation forfeited their liberty in this manner? Whatever individuals have done, yet, I believe, no such challenge can be made upon them as a body. As there should be some rule whereby to govern the conduct of men, so it is the duty and interest of a community to form a system of law that is calculated to promote the commercial interest of each other, and as long as it produces so blessed an effect, it should be maintained. But when, instead of contributing to the well-being of the community, it proves baneful to its subjects over whom it extends, then it is high time to call it in question. Should any ask where we shall find any system of law whereby to regulate our moral conduct, I think there is none so explicit and indefinite as that which was given by the blessed Savior of the world: "Whatsoever ye would that men should do to you: do ye even so to them" (see Matt. 7:12). One would think that the mention of the precept would strike conviction to the heart of these slave traders—unless an avaricious disposition governs the laws of humanity. If we strictly adhere to the rule, we shall not impose anything upon others but what we should be willing to have imposed upon us were we in their condition.

I shall now go on to consider the manner in which the slave trade is carried on, by which it will plainly appear that the practice is vile and atrocious as well as the most inhuman. It is undoubtedly true that those who emigrate slaves from Africa do endeavor to raise mutinies among them in order to procure slaves. Here I would make use of some extracts from a pamphlet printed in Philadelphia a few years ago, the veracity of which need not be scrupled, seeing it agrees with many other accounts.

A. Brue, director of the French factory at Senegal, who lived twenty-seven years in that country, says that "the Europeans are far from desiring to act as peacemakers among the Negros, which would be acting contrary to their interest, since the greater the wars, the more slaves are procured."[1] William Boseman, factor for the Dutch at Delmina, where he resided sixteen years, relates that

> one of the former Commanders hired an army of the Negros of Jefferia and Cabesteria, for a large sum of money, to fight the Negros of Commanry, which occasioned a battle, which

[1] Haynes is quoting Granville Sharp's *Extract from a Representation of the Injustice and Dangerous Tendency of Tolerating Slavery, or Admitting the Least Claim of Private Property in the Persons of Men in England* (London: 1769).

was more bloody than the wars of the Negros usually are, and another Commander gave at one time five hundred pounds, and at another time eight hundred pounds, to two other Negro nations to induce them to take up arms against their country people.[2]

This is confirmed by Barbot, agent general of the French African company, who says,

The Hollanders, a people very zealous for their commerce at the coasts, were very studious to have the war carried on amongst the Blacks to distract, as long as possible, the trade of the other Europeans, and to that effect, were very ready to assist upon all occasions the Blacks, their allies, that they might beat their enemies, and so the commerce fall into their hands.[3]

2   Haynes is quoting Sharp's *Extract*.
3   Haynes is quoting Sharp's *Extract*.

And one William Smith, who was sent by the African company to visit their settlements in the year 1726, from the information he received from one who had resided ten years, said that

> the discerning natives accounted it their greatest unhappiness that they were ever visited by the Europeans—that we Christians introduced the traffic of slaves and that before our coming they lived in peace. But, say they, it is observable that wherever Christianity comes, there comes with it a sword, a gun, powder, and ball.[4]

And thus it brings ignominy upon our holy religion and makes the name of Christians sound odious in the ears of the heathen. O Christianity, how art thou disgraced, how art thou reproached by the vicious practices of those upon whom thou dost smile! Let us go on to consider the great

4   Haynes is quoting Sharp's *Extract*.

hardships and sufferings those slaves are put to in order to be transported into these plantations. There are generally many hundred slaves put on board a vessel and they are shackled together, two by two, worse than criminals going to the place of execution; and they are crowded together as close as possible and almost naked. And their sufferings are so great, as I have been credibly informed, that it often carries off one-third of them on their passage; yea, many have put an end to their own lives for very anguish. And as some have manifested a disposition to rise in their defense, they have been put to the most cruel tortures and deaths as human art could inflict. And oh, the sorrows, the grief, the distress, and anguish that attends them! And not only them but their friends also in their own country when they must forever part with each other! What must be the plaintive notes that the tender parents must assume for the loss of their exiled child? Or the husband for his departed wife? And how do the cries of their departed friends echo from the watery deep! Do not I really hear the fond mother expressing her sorrows in accents that might well pierce the most obdurate heart? "O my child, why, why was thy destiny hung on so precarious a thread! Unhappy fate! Oh, that I were a captive with thee or for thee! Cursed be the day wherein I bare thee, and let that inauspicious night be remembered no more. Come, O king of terrors. Dissipate my grief and send my woes into oblivion."

But I need not stand painting the dreary scene. Let me rather appeal to tender parents whether this is exaggerating matters. Let me ask them what would be their distress should one of their dearest children be snatched from them in a clandestine manner and carried to Africa or some other foreign land to be under the most abject slavery for life, among a strange people. Would it not embitter all your domestic comforts? Would he not be ever upon your mind? Nay, doth not nature even recoil at the reflection?

And are not there many ready to say (unless void of natural affections) that it would not fail to bring them down with sorrow to the grave? And surely, this has been the awful fate of some of those Negros who have been brought into these plantations—which is not to be wondered at, unless we suppose them to be without natural affections, which is to rank them below the very beasts of the field.

Oh, what an immense deal of African blood has been shed by the inhuman cruelty of Englishmen that reside in a Christian land, both at home and in their own country, they being the fomenters of those wars that are absolutely necessary in order to carry on this cursed trade and in their emigration into these colonies and by their merciless masters, in some parts at least! O ye who have made yourselves drunk with human blood! Although you may go with impunity here in this life, yet God will hear the cries of that innocent blood, which cries from the sea and from the ground against you like the blood of Abel, more pealful than thunder, "Vengeance! Vengeance!" What will you do in that day when God shall make inquisition for blood? He will make you drink the vials of his indignation, which like a potable stream shall be poured out without the least mixture of mercy. Believe it, sirs, there shall not a drop of blood that you have spilt unjustly that shall be lost in forgetfulness, but it shall bleed afresh and testify against you in the day when God shall deal with sinners.

We know that under the Levitical economy, man stealing was to be punished with death; so we esteem those who steal any of our earthy commodity guilty of a very heinous crime. What then must be an adequate punishment to be inflicted on those who steal men?

Men were made for more noble ends than to be drove to market like sheep and oxen. "Our being Christians," says one, "does not give us the least liberty to trample on heathen, nor does it give us the least superiority over them." And not only are they guilty of man stealing that are the immediate actors in this trade, but those in these colonies who buy them at their hands are far from being guiltless, for when they saw the thief they consented with him. If men would forbear to buy slaves off the hands of the slave merchants, then the trade would of necessity cease. If I buy a man, whether I am told he was stolen or not, yet I have no right to enslave him because he is a human being, and the immutable laws of God and indefeasible laws of nature pronounced him free.

Is it not exceeding strange that mankind should become such mere vassals to their own carnal avarice as even to imbrue their hands in innocent blood? And to bring such intolerable oppressions upon others that were they themselves to feel them, perhaps they would esteem death preferable. Pray, consider the miseries of a slave, being under the absolute control of another, subject to continual embarrassments, fatigues, and corrections at the will of a master. It is as much impossible for us to bring a man heartily to acquiesce in a passive obedience in this case as it would be to stop a man's breath and yet have it cause no convulsion in nature. Those Negros amongst us who have children, they—namely, their children—are brought up under a partial discipline, their White masters having but little or no affection for them (so that we may suppose that the abuses that they receive from the hands of their masters are often very considerable) and their parents being placed in such a situation as not being able to perform relative duties. Such are those restrictions they are kept under by their taskmasters that they are rendered incapable of performing those moral duties either to God or man that are infinitely binding on all the human race. How often are they separated from each other here in this land at many hundred miles' distance, children from parents and parents from children, husbands from wives and wives from husbands? Those whom God has joined together and pronounced one flesh, man assumes a prerogative to put asunder. What can be more abject than their condition? In short, if I may so speak, it is a hell upon earth; and all this for filthy lucre's sake.

Be astonished, O ye heavens, at this! I believe it would be much better for these colonies if there was never a slave brought into this land, as thereby our poor are put to great extremities by reason of the plentifulness of labor, which otherwise would fall into their hands.

I shall now go on to take under consideration some of those arguments that those who are concerned in the slave trade do use in vindication of their practice, which arguments, I shall endeavor to show, are lame and defective.

The first argument that I shall take notice of is this, namely, that in all probability the Negros are of Canaan's posterity, who were destined by the Almighty to slavery, therefore the practice is warrantable, to which I answer that whether the Negros are of Canaan's posterity or not perhaps is not known by any mortal under heaven, but allowing they were actually of Canaan's posterity, yet we have no reason to think that this curse lasted any longer than the coming of Christ. When that Sun of Righteousness arose, this wall of partition was broken down. Under the law, there were many external ceremonies that were typical of spiritual things or shadowed forth the purity and perfection of the gospel as corporeal blemishes. Spurious birth and flagitious practices debarred them from the congregation of the Lord, thereby showing the intrinsic purity of heart that a concealed gospel required as the prerequisite for heaven, as Ham uncovered his father's nakedness, that is, did not endeavor to conceal it but gazed perhaps with a lascivious eye, which was repugnant to the law that was afterward given to the children of Israel. So it was most necessary that God should manifest his signal disapprobation of this heinous sin by making him and his posterity a public example to the world that thereby they might be set apart and separated from the people of God as unclean. And we find it was a privilege granted to God's people of old that they might enslave the heathen and the stranger that were in the land, thereby to show the superior privileges God's people enjoyed above the rest of the world, so that us Gentiles were then subject to slavery, being then heathen. If they will keep close to the letter they must own themselves yet subject to the yoke, unless we suppose them free by being brought into the same place or having the same privileges with the Jews. Then it follows that we may enslave all nations, be they White or Black, that are heathens, which they themselves will not allow. We find under that dispensation God declaring that he would visit "the iniquity of the fathers upon the children . . . unto the third and fourth generation" (Ex. 34:7). And we find it so in the case of Ham as well as many others, their posterity being extrinsically unclean.

But now our glorious high priest has visibly appeared in the flesh and has established a more glorious economy. He has not only visibly broken down that wall of partition that interposed between the offended majesty of heaven and rebellious sinners and removed those tedious forms under the law that savored so much of servitude and could never make the comers thereunto perfect by rendering them obsolete, but he has also removed those many embarrassments and distinctions that they were incident to under so contracted a dispensation so that whatever bodily imperfections or whatever birth we sustain, it does not in the least debar us from gospel privileges or whatever heinous practice any may be guilty of. Yet if they manifest a gospel repentance, we have no right to debar them from our communion.

And it is plain beyond all doubt that at the coming of Christ, this curse that was upon Canaan was taken off. And I think there is not less force in this argument than there would be to argue that an imperfect contexture of parts or base birth should deprive any from gospel privileges or bring up any of those antiquated ceremonies from oblivion and reduce them into practice.

But you will say that slave keeping was practiced even under the gospel, for we find Paul and the other apostles exhorting servants to be obedient to their masters, to which I reply that it might be they were speaking to servants in minority in general, but doubtless it was practiced in the days of the apostles from what Saint Paul says in 1 Corinthians 7:21, "Art thou called being a servant? care not for it; but if thou mayest be made free, use it rather," so that the apostle seems to recommend freedom if attainable. It is as if he says, "if it is thy unhappy lot to be a slave, yet if thou art spiritually free let the former appear so minute a thing when compared with the latter that it is comparatively unworthy of notice; yet since freedom is so excellent a jewel, which none have a right to extirpate, and if there is any hope of attaining it, use all lawful measures for that purpose," so that however extant or prevalent it might be in that or this age, yet it does not in the least reverse the unchangeable laws of God or of nature or make that become lawful which is in itself unlawful, neither is it strange if we consider the moral depravity of man's nature throughout all ages of the world that mankind should deviate from the unerring rules of heaven.

But again, another argument that some use to maintain their intolerable oppression upon others is this, namely, that those Negros who are brought into these plantations are generally prisoners, taken in their wars, and would otherwise fall sacrifice to the resentment of their own people. But this argument, I think, is plainly confuted by the aforecited account that Mr. Boseman gives, as well as many others. Again, some say they came honestly by their slaves because they bought them of their parents (that is, those who brought them from Africa) and rewarded them well for them. Without doubt this is, for the most part, false. But allowing they did actually buy them of their parents, yet I query whether parents have any right to sell their children for slaves: if parents have a right to be free, then it follows that their children have equally as good a right to their freedom, even hereditarily. So, to use the words of a learned writer,

one has nobody to blame but himself in case he shall find himself deprived of a man whom he thought by buying for a price he had made his own, for he dealt in a trade that was illicit and was prohibited by the most obvious dictates of humanity. For these reasons, every one of those unfortunate men, who are pretended to be slaves, have a right to be declared free, for he never lost his liberty; he could not lose it; his prince had no power to dispose of him. Of course the sale was *ipso jure* void.[5]

But I shall take notice of one argument more that these slave traders use, and it is this, namely, that those Negros who are emigrated into these colonies are brought out of a land of darkness under the meridian light of the gospel; and so it is a great blessing instead of a curse. But I would ask, "Who is this that darkeneth counsel by words without knowledge?" (Job 38:2). Let us attend to the great apostle speaking to us in Romans 3:8

5 Haynes is quoting George Wallace, *A System of the Principles of the Law of Scotland* (Edinburgh: 1760).

where he reproves some slanderers who told it as
a maxim preached by the apostles that they said,
"Let us do evil, that good may come[,] whose
damnation," the inspired penman pronounces
with an emphasis, "is just." And again, Romans
6:1, whereby way of interrogation he asks, "Shall
we continue in sin, that grace may abound?"
The answer is obvious: "God forbid" (v. 2). But
that those slave merchants who trade upon the
coasts of Africa do not aim at the spiritual good
of their slaves is evident by their behavior toward them; if they had their spiritual good at
heart, we should expect that those slave merchants who trade upon their coasts would, instead of causing quarrellings and bloodshed
among them (which is repugnant to Christianity and below the character of humanity), be
solicitous to demean exemplary among them,
that by their wholesome conduct, those heathen

might be induced to entertain high and admiring thoughts of our holy religion. Those slaves in these colonies are generally kept under the greatest ignorance and blindness, and they are scarcely ever told by their White masters whether there is a Supreme Being who governs the universe or whether there is any reward or punishment beyond the grave. Nay, such are those restrictions that they are kept under that they scarcely know that they have a right to be free, or if they do, they are not allowed to speak in their defense. Such is their abject condition that that genius that is peculiar to the human race cannot have that cultivation that the polite world is favored with and therefore they are styled the ignorant part of the world, whereas had they the same advantages to get knowledge with them, perhaps their progress in arts would not be inferior.

But should we give ourselves the trouble to inquire into the grand motive that indulges men to concern themselves in a trade so vile and abandon, we shall find it to be this, namely, to stimulate their carnal avarice and to maintain men in pride, luxury, and idleness. And how much it has subserved to this vile purpose I leave the candid public to judge. I speak it with reverence yet I think all must give in that it has such a tendency.

But although God is of long patience, yet it does not last always; nay, he has whet his glittering sword and his hand has already taken hold on judgment. For who knows how far that the unjust oppression that has abounded in this land may be the procuring cause of this very judgment that now impends, which so much portends slavery. For this is God's way of working. Often he brings the same judgments or evils upon men as they unrighteously bring upon others, as is plain from Judges 1:6–7, "But Adonibezek fled; and they pursued after him, and caught him, and cut off his thumbs and his great toes. And Adonibezek said, Threescore and ten kings, having their thumbs and their great toes cut off, gathered their meat under my table: as I have done, so God has requited me." And as wicked Ahab and Jezebel, to gratify their covetousness, caused Naboth to be put to death, and as dogs licked the blood of Naboth, the word of the Lord was by the prophet Elijah, "Thus saith the LORD, in the place where dogs licked the blood of Naboth shall dogs lick thy blood, even thine" (1 Kings 21:19). And "of Jezebel also spake the LORD, saying, The dogs shall eat Jezebel by the walls of Jezreel" (v. 23). And we find the judgment actually accomplished upon Ahab in 1 Kings 22:38 and upon Jezebel in 2 Kings 9. Again, Revelation 16:6, "For they have shed the blood of saints and prophets, and thou hast given them blood to drink; for they are worthy." And Revelation 18:6, "Reward her even as she rewarded you." I say this is often God's way of dealing, by retaliating back upon men the same evils that they unjustly bring upon others. I don't say that we have reason to think that oppression is the alone cause of this judgment that God is pleased to bring upon this land, nay. But we have the greatest reason to think that this is not one of the least. And whatever some may think—that I am instigated by a false zeal and all that I have said upon the subject is mere novelty—yet I am not afraid to appeal to the conscience of any rational and honest man as to the truth of what I have just hinted at. And if any will not confide in what I have humbly offered, I am persuaded it must be such shortsighted persons whose contracted eyes never penetrate through the narrow confines of self and are mere vassals to filthy lucre.

But I cannot persuade myself to write a period to this small treatise without humbly addressing myself more particularly unto all such as are concerned in the practice of slave keeping.

Sirs, should I pursue the dictates of nature, resulting from a sense of my own inability, I should be far from attempting to form this address. Nevertheless, I think that a mere superficial reflection upon the merits of the cause may serve as an ample apology for this humble attempt. Therefore hoping you will take it well at my hands, I presume (though with the greatest submission) to crave your attention while I offer you a few words.

Perhaps you will think the preceding pages unworthy of speculation. Well, let that be as it will. I would solicit you seriously to reflect on your conduct, whether you are not guilty of unjust oppression. Can you wash your hands and say, "I am clean from this sin"? Perhaps you will dare to say it before men; but dare you say it before the tremendous tribunal of that God before whom we must all, in a few precarious moments, appear? Then whatever fair glosses we may have put upon our conduct, that God whose eyes pervade the utmost extent of human thought and surveys with one intuitive view the affairs of men will examine into the matter himself and will set everything upon its own basis, and impartiality shall be seen flourishing throughout that solemn assembly. Alas! Shall men hazard their precious souls for a little of the transitory things of time? O sirs! Let that pity and compassion that are peculiar to mankind, especially to Englishmen, no longer lie dormant in your breast. Let it run free through disinterested benevolence; then how these iron yokes would spontaneously fall from the gauled necks of the oppressed! And that disparity in point of natural privilege, which is the bane of society, would be cast upon the utmost coasts of oblivion. If this was the impulsive exercise that animated all your actions, your consciences would be the only standard unto which I need appeal. Think it neither uncharitable nor censorious to say that whenever we erect our battery so as it is like to prove a detriment to the interest of any, we lose their attention, or if we don't entirely lose that, yet if true Christian candor is wanting we cannot be in a suitable frame for speculation, so that the good effect that these otherwise might have will prove abortive. If I could once persuade you to reflect upon the matter with a single and impartial eye, I am almost assured that no more needs to be said upon the subject. But whether I shall be so happy as to persuade you to cherish such an exercise I know not. Yet I think it is very obvious

from what I have humbly offered that so far forth
as you have been concerned in the slave trade, so
far it is that you have assumed an oppressive and
tyrannic power. Therefore, is it not high time to
undo these heavy burdens and let the oppressed
go free? And while you manifest such a noble and
magnanimous spirit to maintain inviolably your
own natural rights and militate so much against
despotism as it has respect unto yourselves, you
do not assume the same usurpations and are no
less tyrannic. Pray let there be a congruity amidst
your conduct, lest you fall amongst that class the
inspired penman speaks of:

> Thou therefore which teacheth another, teachest
> thou not thyself? thou that preachest a man
> should not steal, dost thou steal? Thou that say-
> est a man should not commit adultery, dost thou
> commit adultery? thou that abhoreth idols, dost

thou commit sacrilege? Thou that makest thy boast of the law, through breaking the law dishonorest thou God? (Rom. 2:21–23)

While you thus sway your tyrant scepter over others, you have nothing to expect but to share in the bitter pill. It was an excellent note that I lately read in a modern piece, and it was this: "Oh, when shall America be consistently engaged in the cause of liberty!"[6] If you have any love to yourselves or any love to this land, if you have any love to your fellow men, break these intolerable yokes and let their names be remembered no more, lest they be retorted on your own necks and you sink under them, for God will not hold you guiltless.

---

6   Haynes is quoting Levi Hart's *Liberty Described and Reccomended; in a Sermon, Preached to the Corporation of Freemen in Farmington, at Their Meeting on Tuesday, September 20, 1774, and Published at Their Desire* (Hartford: 1775).

Sirs, the important cause in which you are engaged in is of an excellent nature; it is ornamental to your characters, and will, undoubtedly, immortalize your names through the latest posterity. And it is pleasing to behold that patriotic zeal that fires your breast. But it is strange that you should want the least stimulation to further expressions of so noble a spirit. Some gentlemen have determined to contend in a consistent manner: they have "let the oppressed go free" (Isa. 58:6).[7]

---

7 After an incomplete sentence ("and I cannot think it is for the want of such a generous principle in you, but through some inadvertency that"), the manuscript ends here.

Scripture Index

Scripture Index

**CROSSWAY SHORT
CLASSICS**

FOR MORE INFORMATION, VISIT **CROSSWAY.ORG**.